HOUND of THE FAR SIDE

Other Books in The Far Side Series

The Far Side
Beyond The Far Side
In Search of The Far Side
Bride of The Far Side
Valley of The Far Side
It Came From The Far Side

Anthologies

The Far Side Gallery
The Far Side Gallery 2

HOUND of THE FAR SIDE
by Gary Larson

Andrews, McMeel & Parker
A Universal Press Syndicate Affiliate
Kansas City • New York

ISBN: 0-8362-2087-0
Library of Congress Catalog Card Number: 87-70296

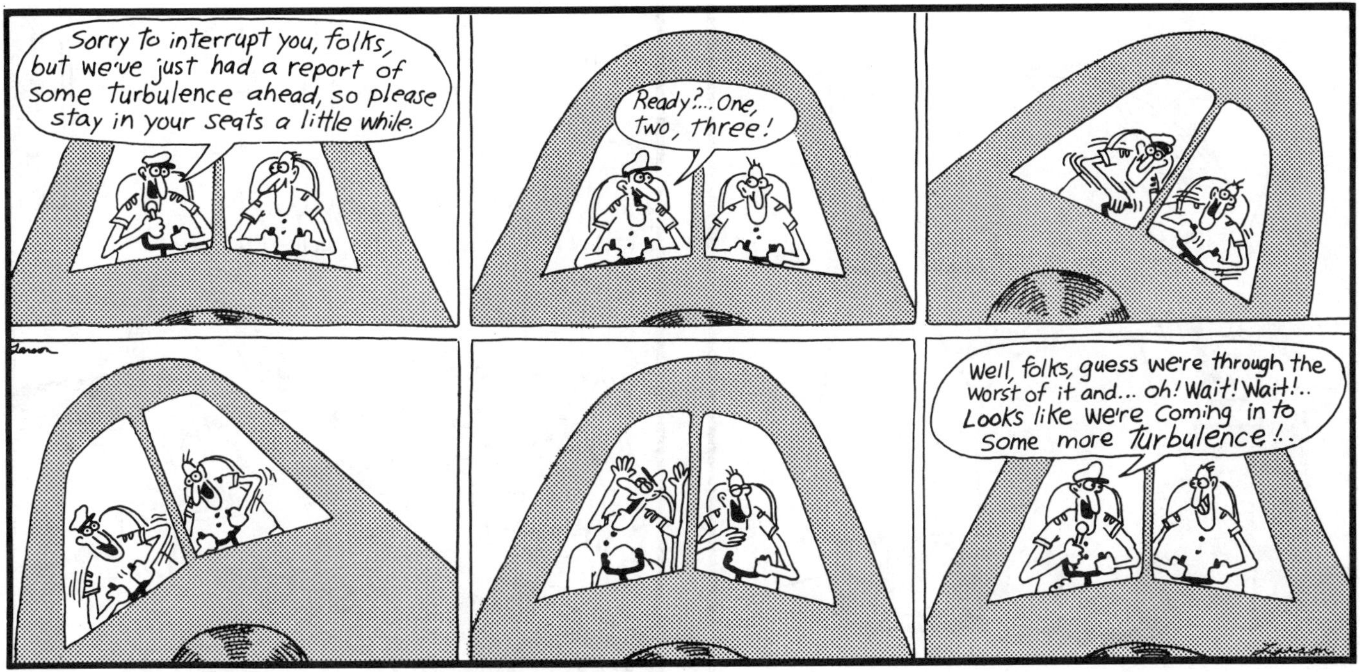
Sorry to interrupt you, folks, but we've just had a report of some turbulence ahead, so please stay in your seats a little while.
Ready?... One, two, three!
Well, folks, guess we're through the worst of it and... oh! Wait! Wait!.. Looks like we're coming in to some more Turbulence!..

"Whoa! *That* was a good one! Try it, Hobbs — just poke his brain right where my finger is."

"We're gettin' old, Jake."

6

"OK, OK, you guys have had your chance — the horses want another shot at it."

Beginning duck

7

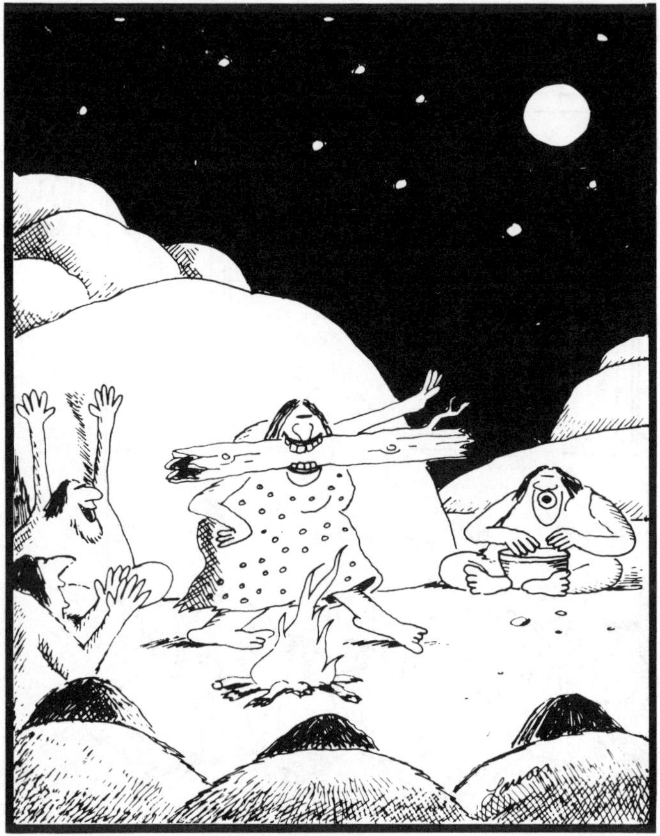
Larson

Primitive fandango

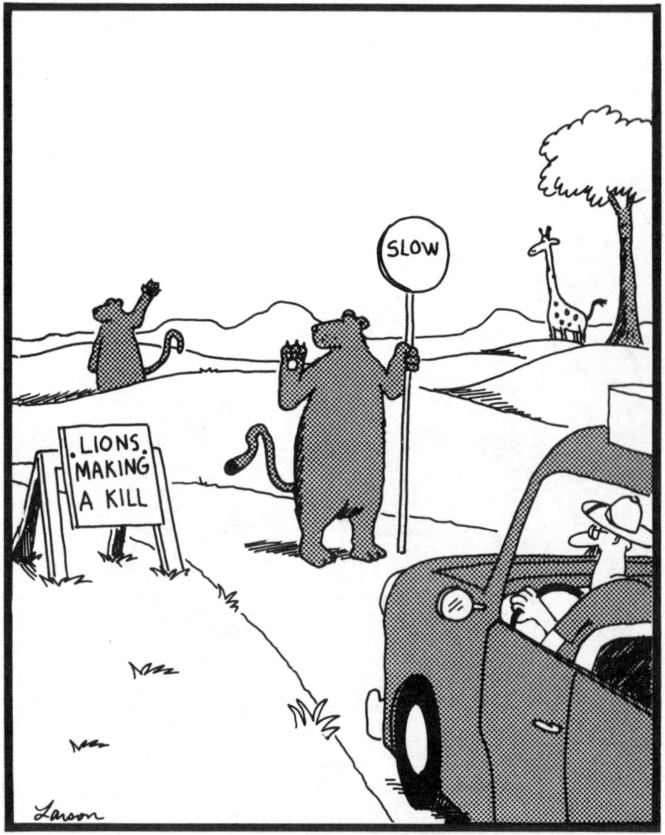
SLOW
LIONS MAKING A KILL
Larson

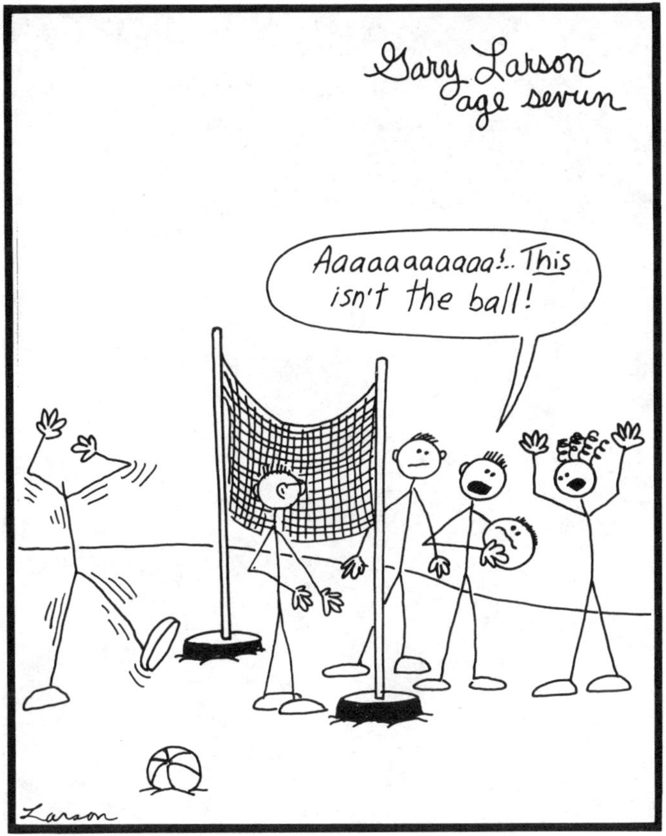
Gary Larson age sevun
Aaaaaaaaaaa!.. This isn't the ball!
Larson

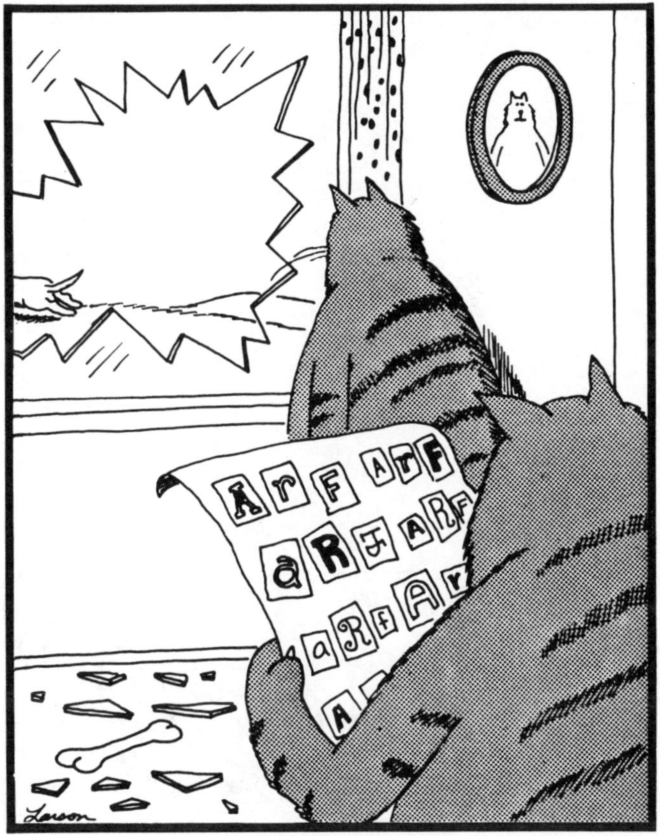
Larson

Dog threat letters

"Uh-oh! ... Stuart blew his air sac!"

Amoeba porn flicks

"Oh, for heaven's sake! Your father left in such a hurry this morning he's lost another antenna."

"Goldberg, you idiot! Don't play tricks on those things —
they can't distinguish between 'laughing with' and
'laughing at'!"

"Hold it right there, Doreen! ... Leave if you must — but
the dog *stays*!"

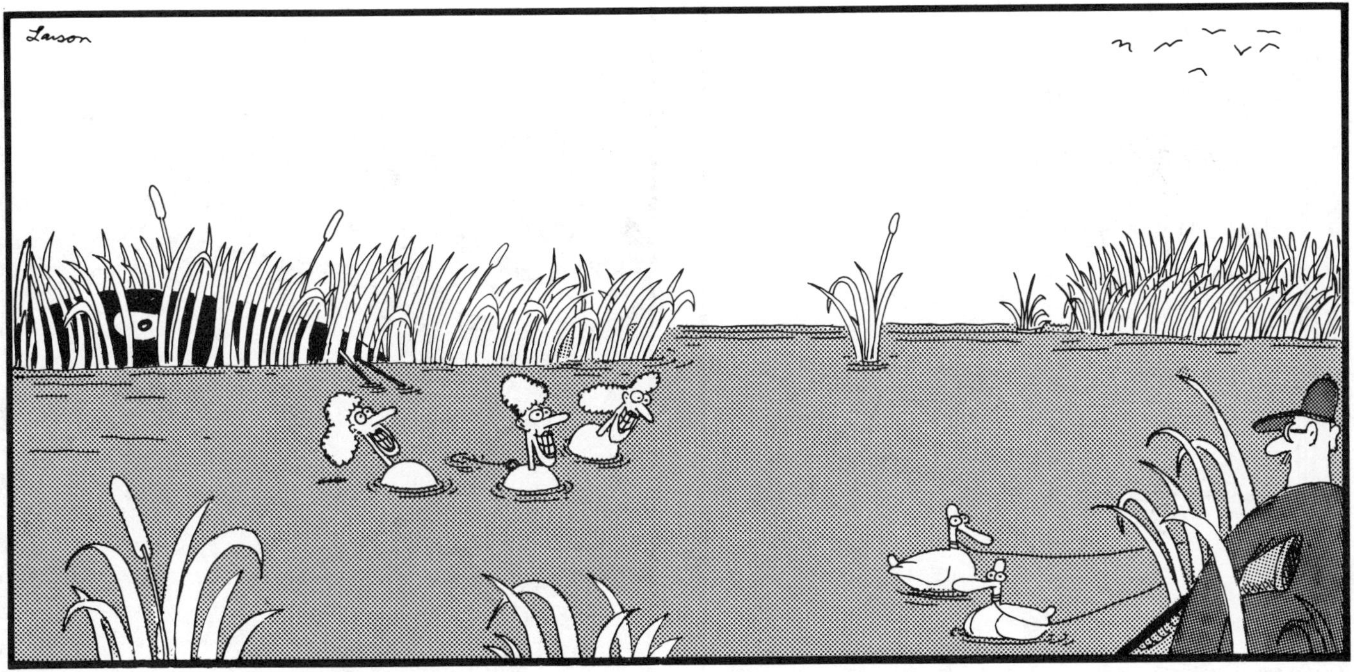
Larson

"Gee, that's a wonderful sensation. ... Early in the morning, you just woke up, you're tired, movin' kinda slow, and then that ooooold smell hits your nose ... blood in the water."

"Here comes another big one, Roy, and here — we — gooooooowheeeeeeeoooo!"

Rock Shop 101

15

"OK, let's take a look at you."

Early Man

16

Cow joyrides

"Think about it, Ed. ... The class Insecta contains 26 orders, almost 1,000 families, and over 750,000 described species — but I can't shake the feeling we're all just a bunch of bugs."

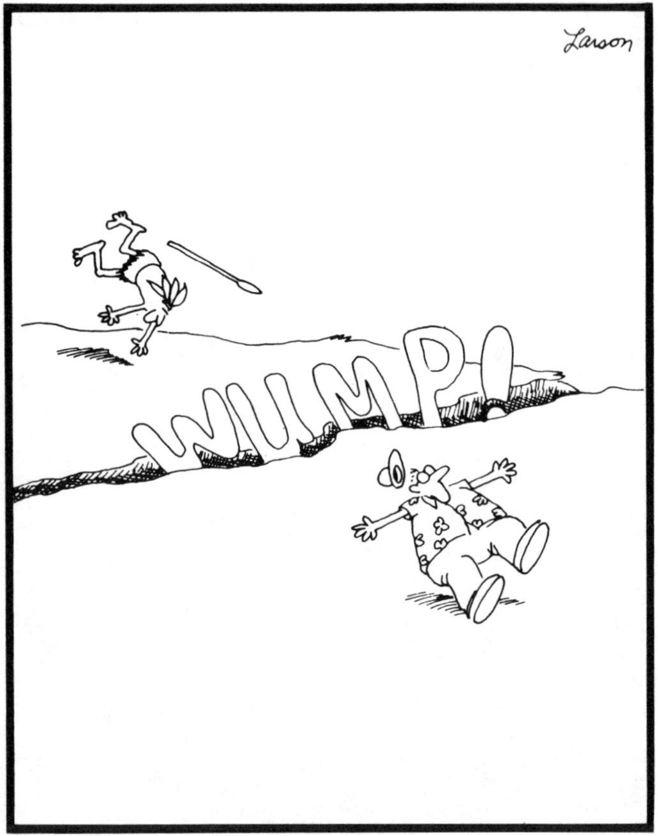
WUMP!

Continental drift whiplash

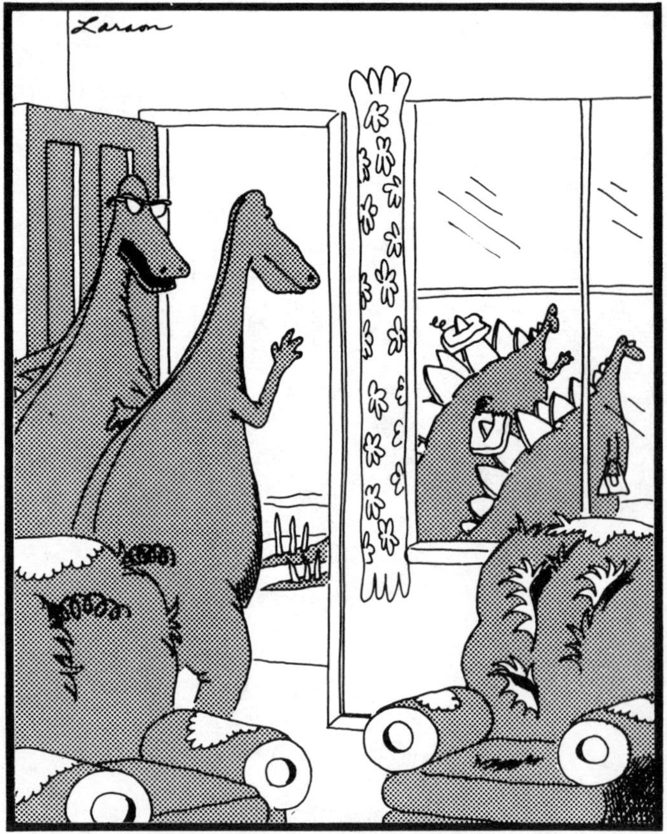

"Well, that does it! Look at our furniture! The Shuelers have visited us for the last time!"

"Donald ... Trade you a thorax and six legs for two of your segments."

"Second floor, please."

"Well, I'll be ... Honey, it's the Worthingtons — our favorite couple of slimebags."

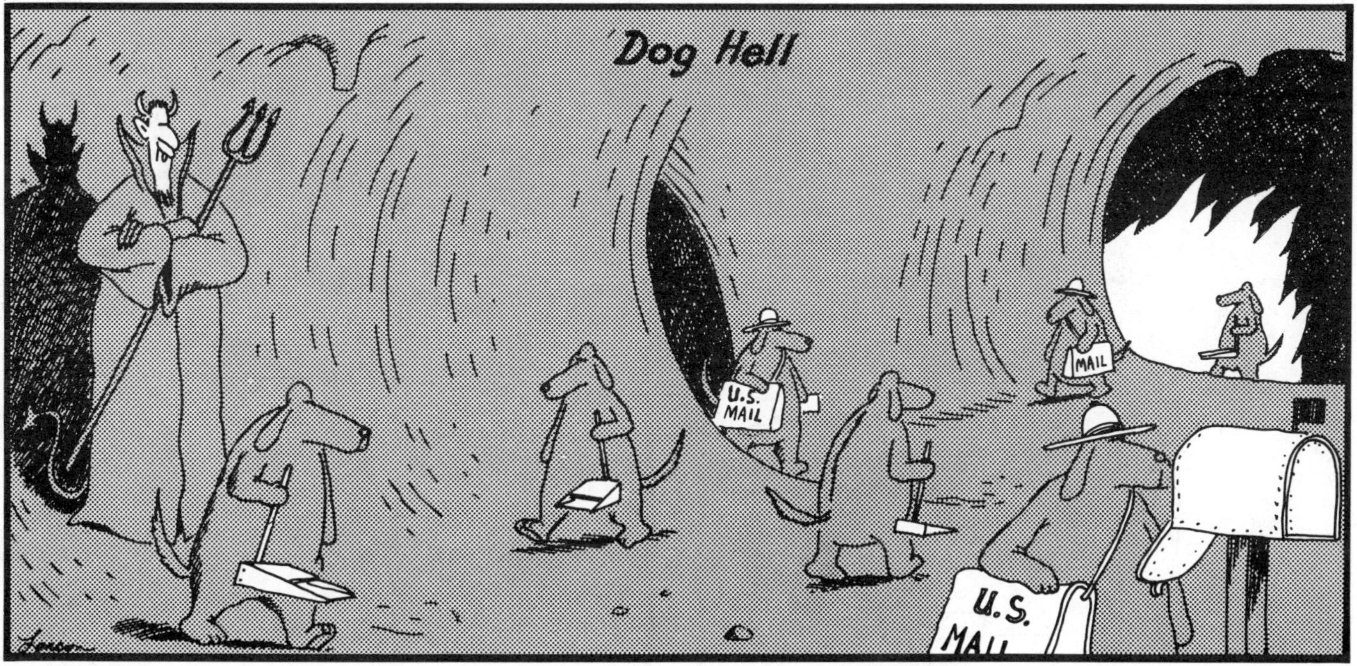
Dog Hell
U.S. MAIL
MAIL
U.S. MAIL

In God's den

The secret python burial grounds

"Dang, that gives me the creeps. ... I wish she'd hurry up and scoop that guy out."

"You idiot! We want the scent on the pillow!
On the pillow!"

"I'm *talking* to you! ... You're so ... so ... so thick-
membraned sometimes."

"And here we are last summer off the coast of ... Helen,
is this Hawaii or Florida?"

"Wait a minute, Vince! Last summer — remember? Some little kid caught you, handled you, and tossed you back in the swamp ... *That's* where you got 'em."

Unknown to most historians, William Tell had an older and less fortunate son named Warren.

25

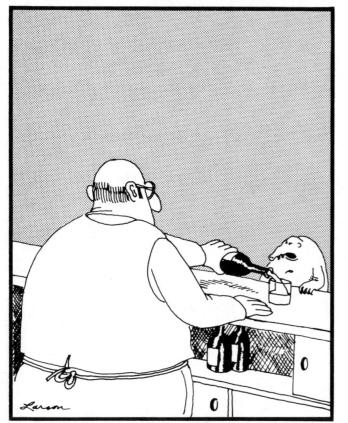

"Sho I sez to her, 'Hey, look! I'm tired of living in this hole, digging dirt, and eating worms!'"

The old "fake harpoon" gag

"Well, sorry about this, Mrs. Murdoch, but old Roy and I got to arguin' politics, and dang if he didn't say some things that got my adrenalin flowin'."

27

Going out for the evening, Tarzan and Jane forget to tie up the dog.

WORMTALK
And
SLUGSPEAK
My Life Among
the Invertebrates
by Prof. [illegible]

About the Author

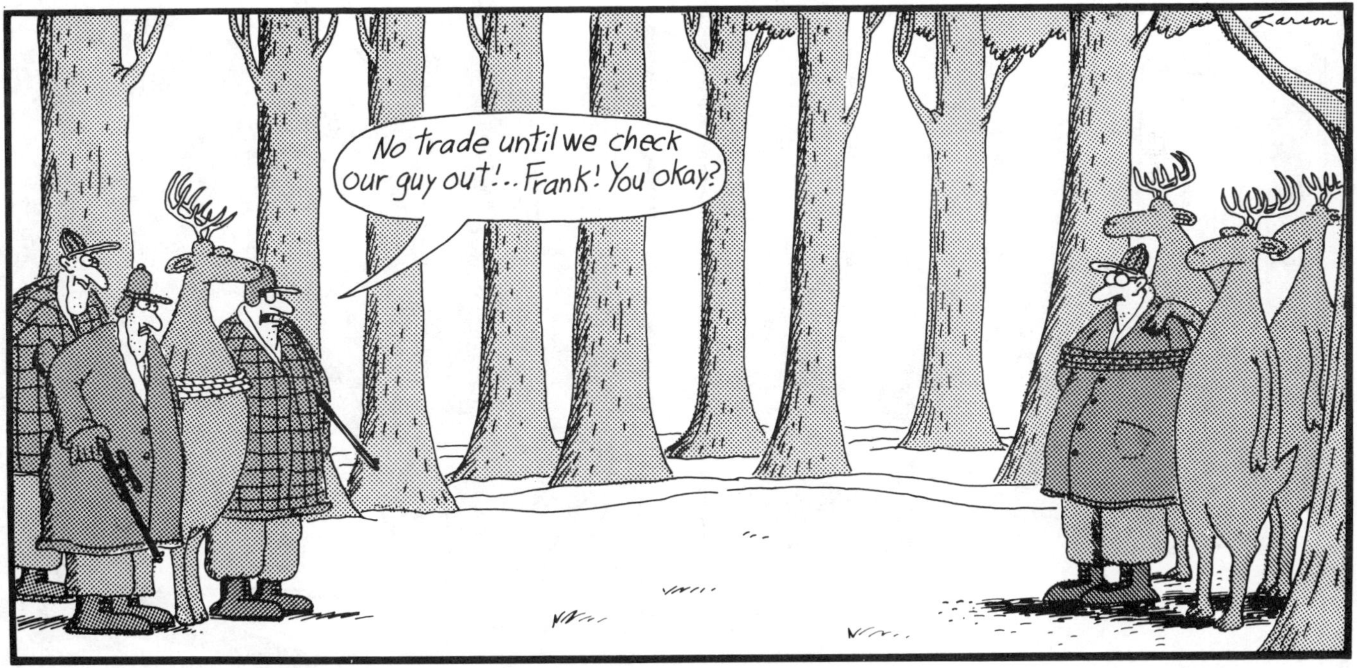
No trade until we check our guy out!.. Frank! You okay?
Larson

"Uh-oh, Norm. Across the street — whale-watchers."

An impressionable moment in the childhood
of Buffalo Bill

"Nik! The fireflies across the street — I think they're
mooning us!"

"No, he's not busy ... In fact, that whole thing
is just a myth."

"Margaret! He's doing it! He's doing it!"

Elephant campfires

"Now, here's a feature you folks would really enjoy ...
Voila! A tree right off the master bedroom."

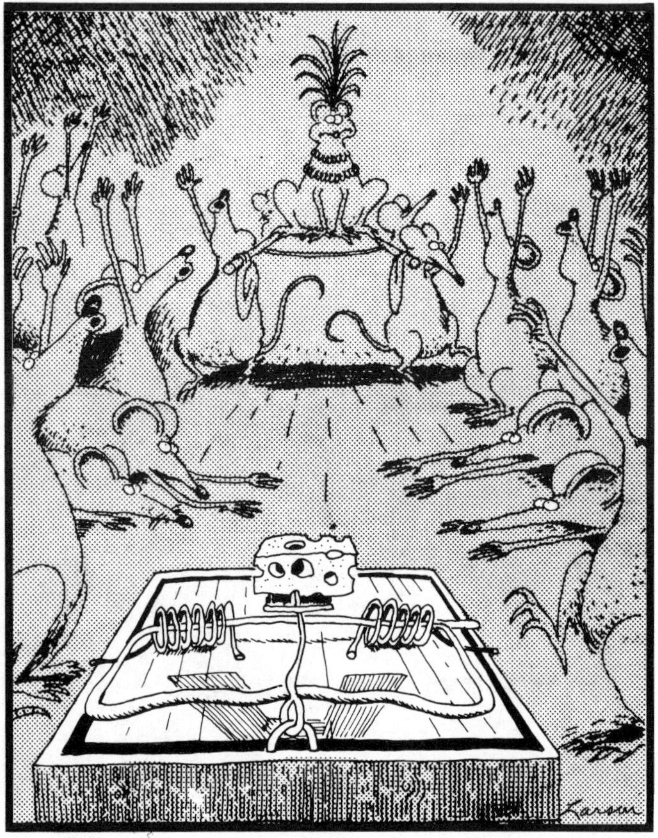
Larson

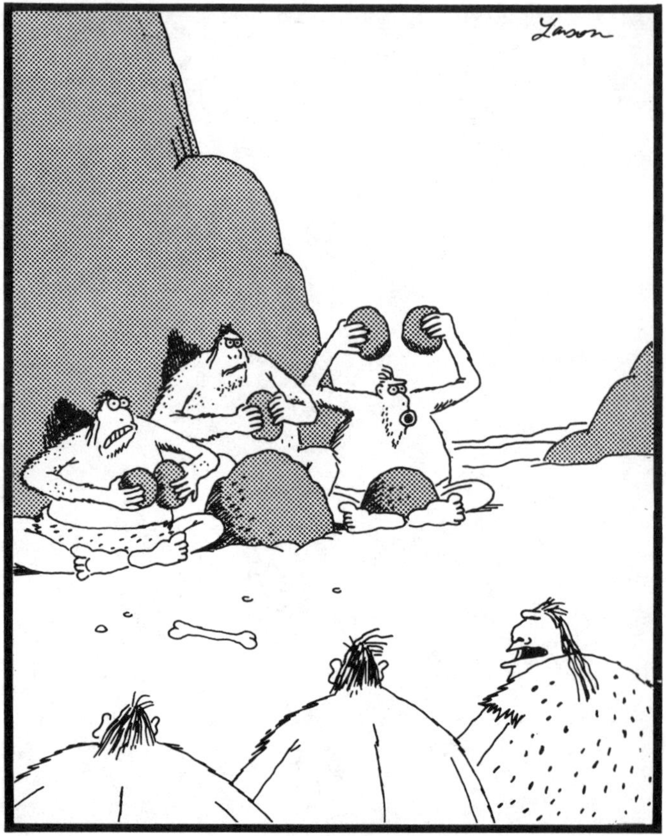
Larson

"Grog ... They play our song."

Same planet, different worlds

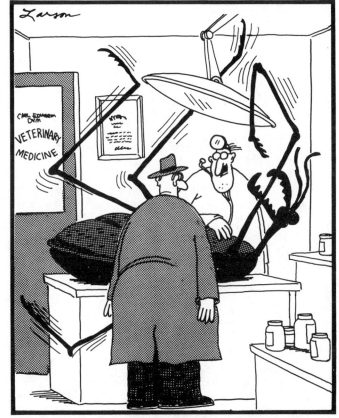

"I'm sorry, Mr. Caldwell, but the big guy's on his way out. If you want my opinion, take him home, find a quiet spot out in the yard, and squash him."

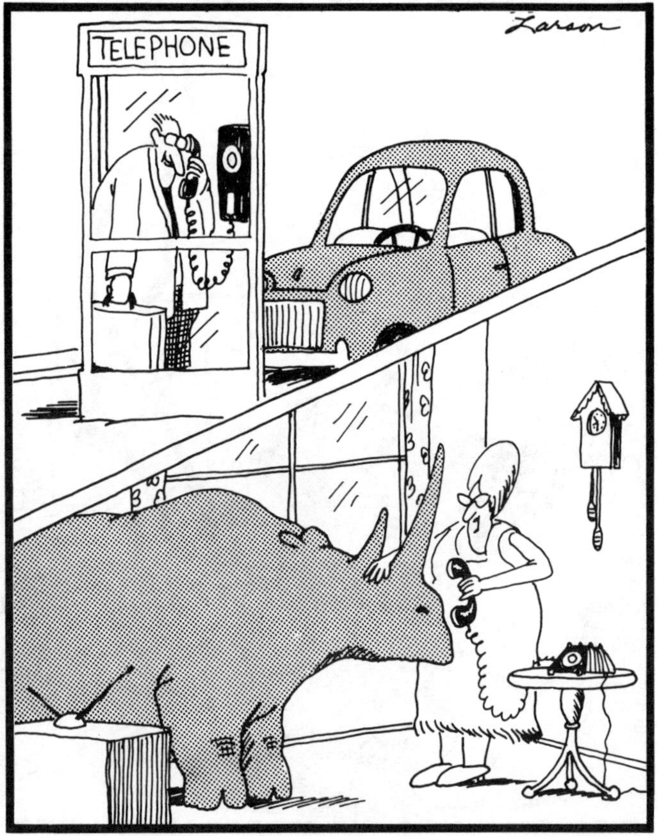
Larson
TELEPHONE
"Come on, baby … One grunt for Daddy … one grunt for Daddy."

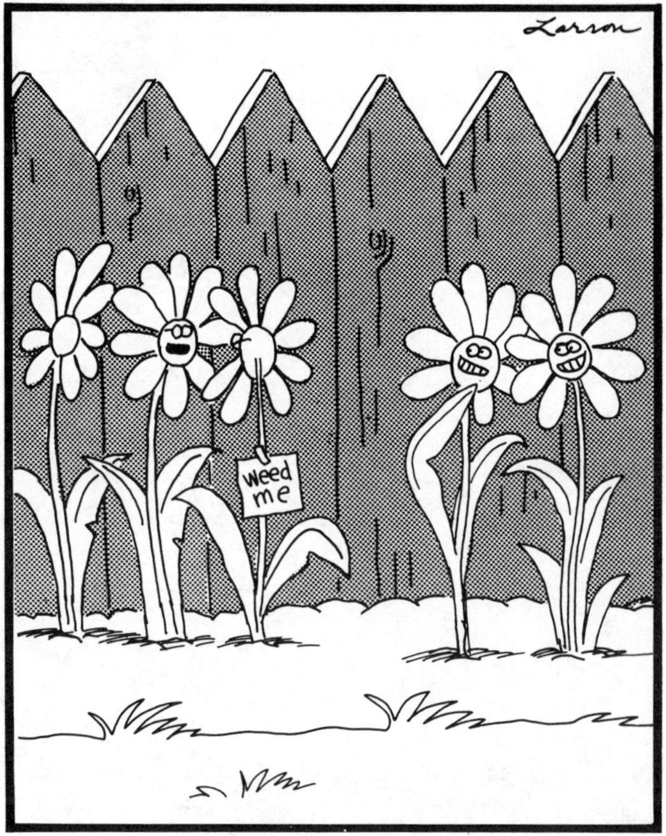
Larson
weed me
Flora practical jokes

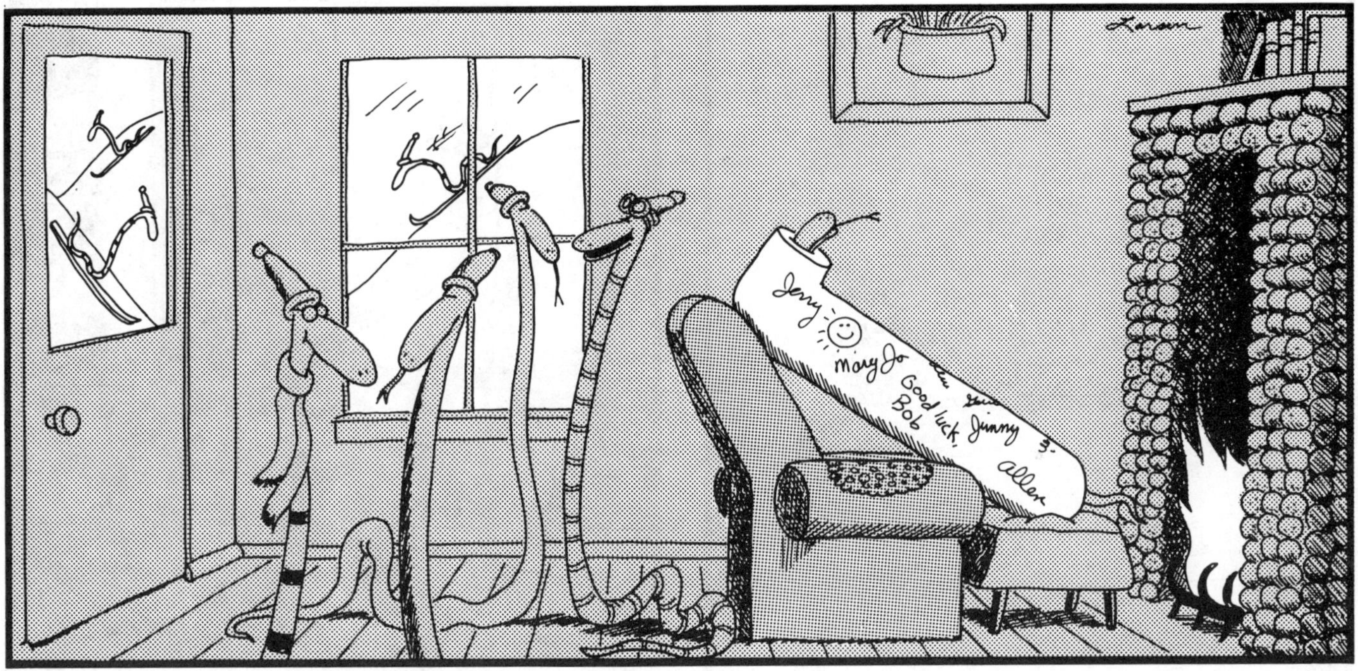
Larson
Jerry
Mary Jo
Good luck, Bob
Jimmy
allen

"I don't mean to exacerbate this situation, Roger, but I think I'm quite close to bursting into maniacal laughter and imagining your nose is really a German sausage."

"It's back, Arnie! Get the book! ... We're gonna settle whether it's an alligator or a crocodile once and for all!"

"Larry? Betty? ... Stand up, will ya? ... These are some friends of mine, folks, who flew all the way in from the dump."

"Doesn't have buck teeth, doesn't have buck teeth, doesn't have..."

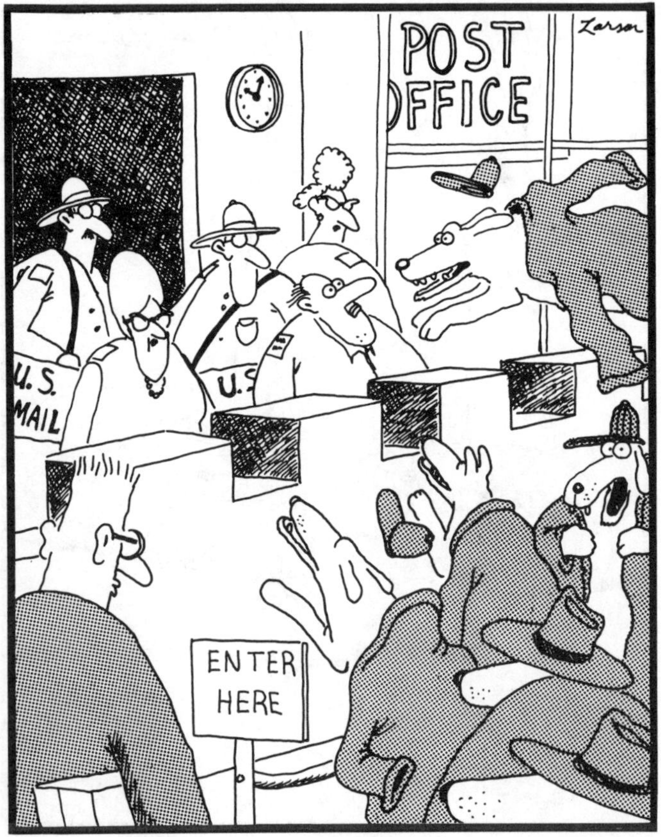
Larson
POST
OFFICE
U.S.
MAIL
U.S
ENTER
HERE

"Now!"

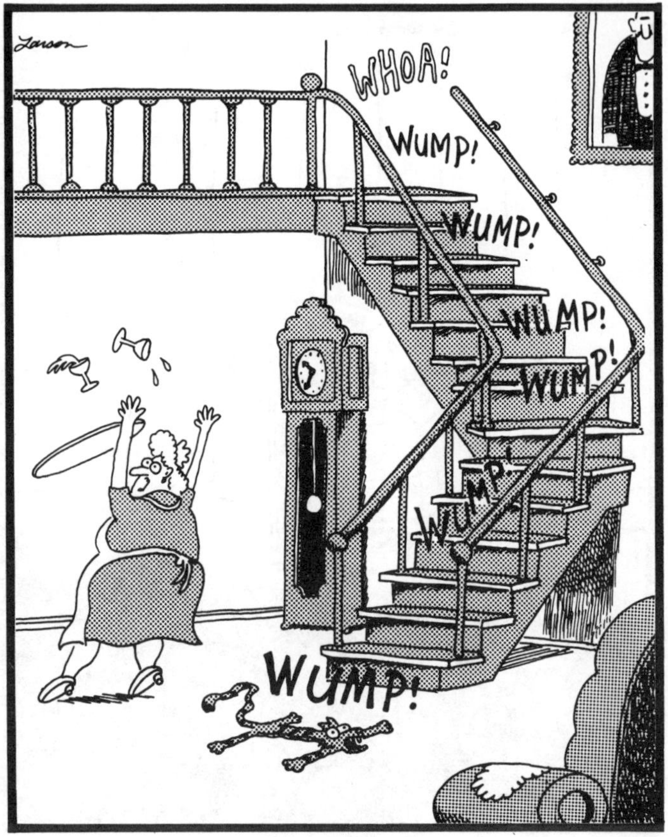
Larson
WHOA!
WUMP!
WUMP!
WUMP!
WUMP!
WUMP!
WUMP!
WUMP!

Clumsy ghosts

"Remember the ... uh ... Remember the ... Remember that place in Texas!"

"You know, I wish you'd get rid of that hideous thing — and I think it's just plain dangerous to have one in the house."

"So tell us, Buffy ... How long have you been a talking dog?"

Before paper and scissors

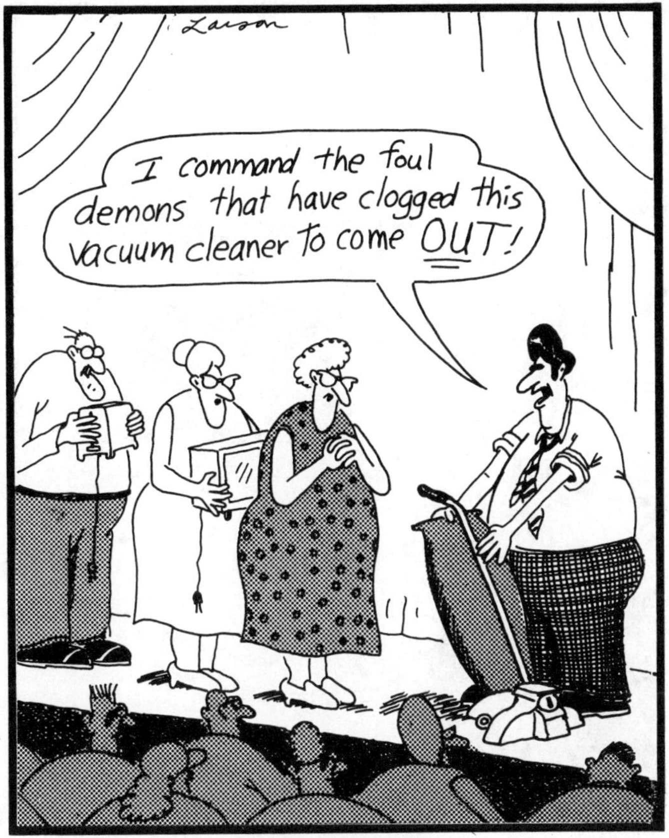
Larson
I command the foul demons that have clogged this vacuum cleaner to come OUT!

Appliance healers

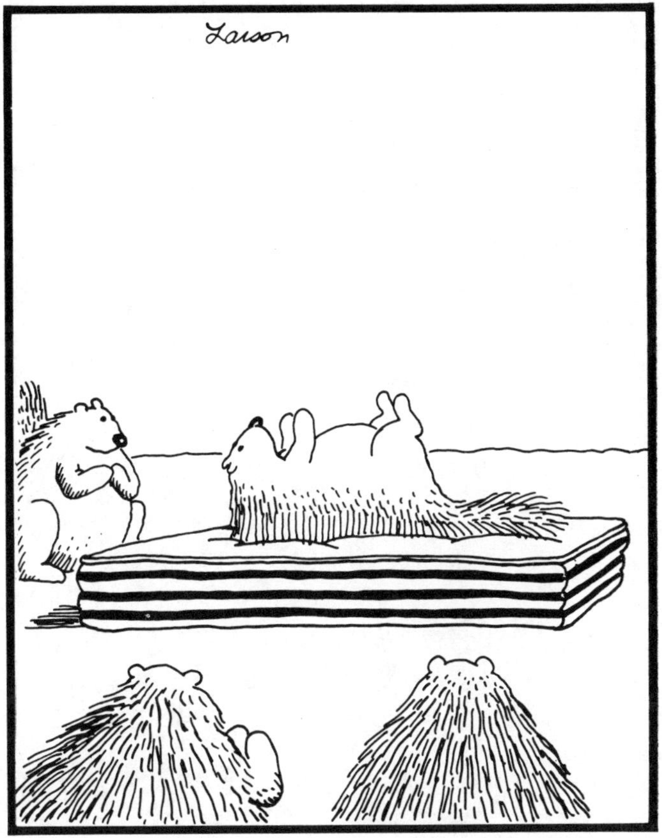
Larson

Another case of too many scientists and not
enough hunchbacks

"Gad, that's eerie ... no matter where you stand the nose
seems to follow."

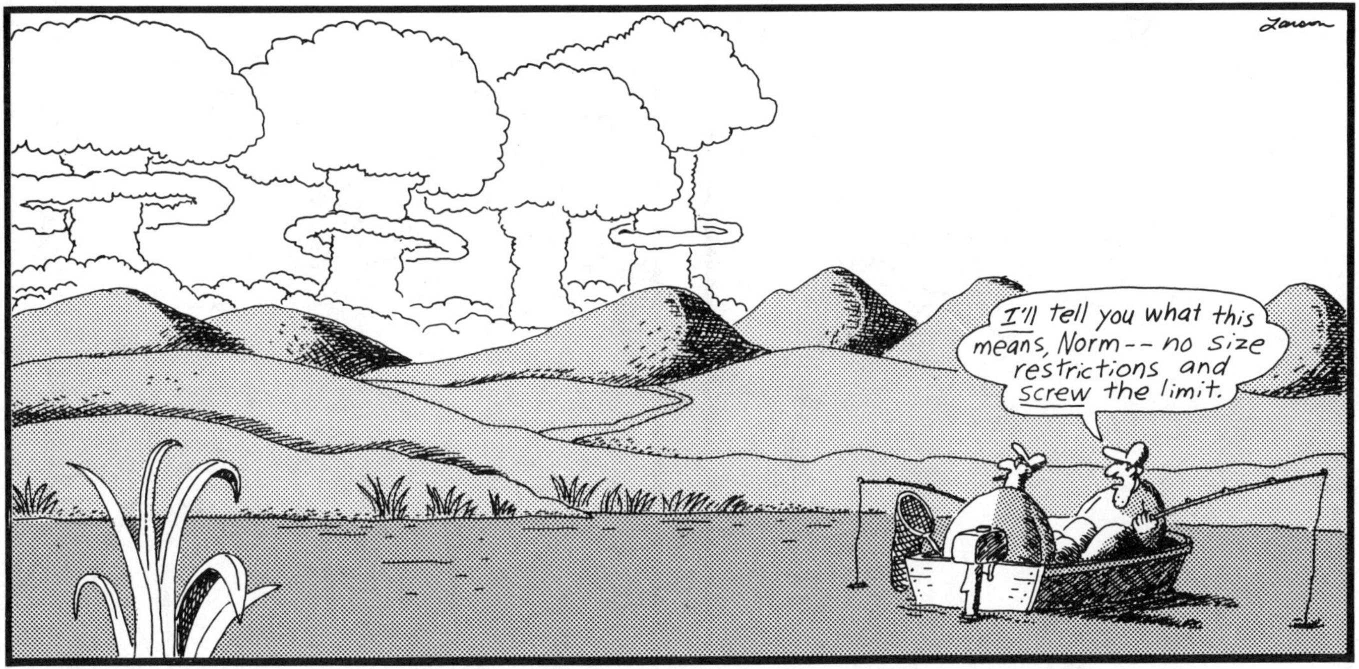
Larson
I'll tell you what this means, Norm-- no size restrictions and screw the limit.

"Looks like some drifter comin' into town."

"Maybe we should write that spot down."

Testing whether fish have feelings

"Hey c'mon! Don't put your mouth on it!"

"Yes, yes ... now don't fuss ... I have something for you all."

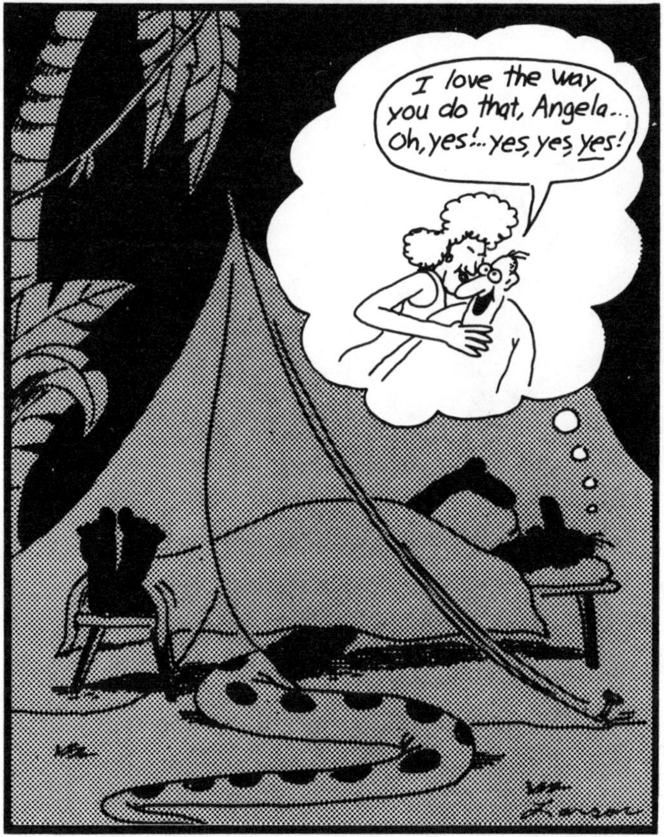
I love the way you do that, Angela... Oh, yes!... yes, yes, yes!
Larson

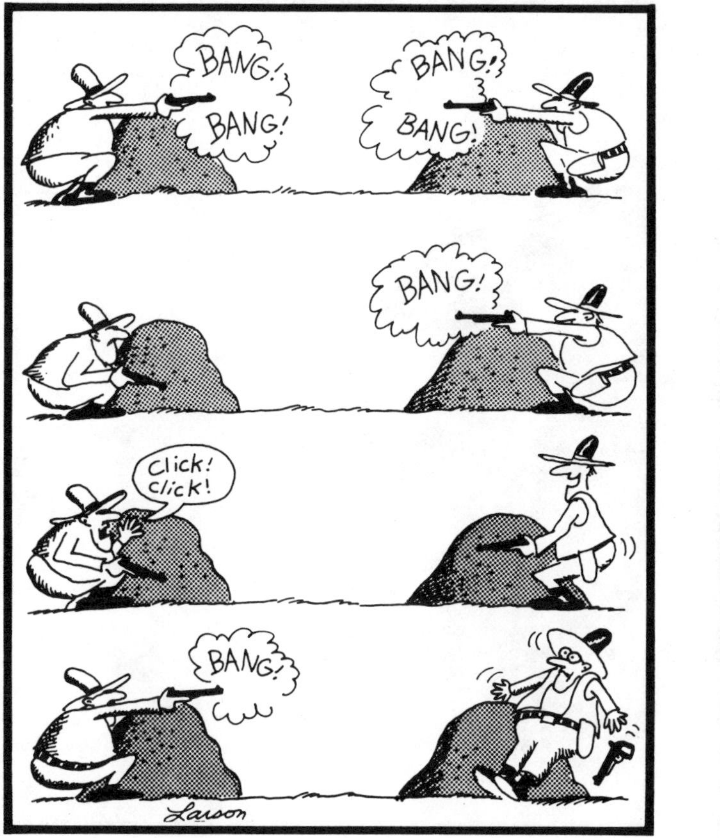
BANG!
BANG!
BANG!
BANG!
BANG!
Click! click!
BANG!
Larson

The primitive game of "Kiss-the-mammoth-and-run"

"Because it's not there."

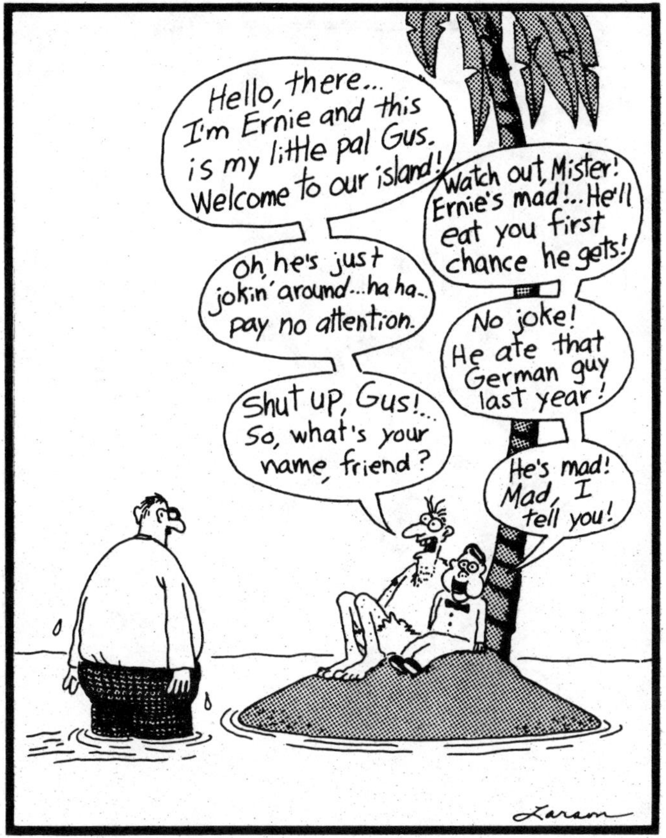
Hello, there... I'm Ernie and this is my little pal Gus. Welcome to our island!
Watch out, Mister! Ernie's mad!... He'll eat you first chance he gets!
Oh, he's just jokin' around... ha ha.. pay no attention.
No joke! He ate that German guy last year!
Shut up, Gus!... So, what's your name, friend?
He's mad! Mad, I tell you!
Larson

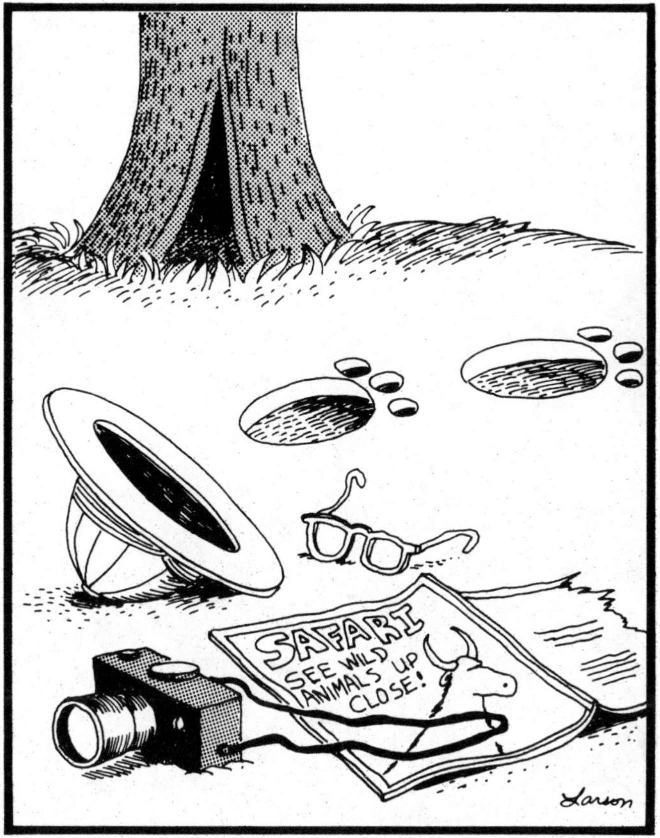
SAFARI
SEE WILD ANIMALS UP CLOSE!
Larson

"Well, that does it for my tomatoes."

Headhunter hall closets

52

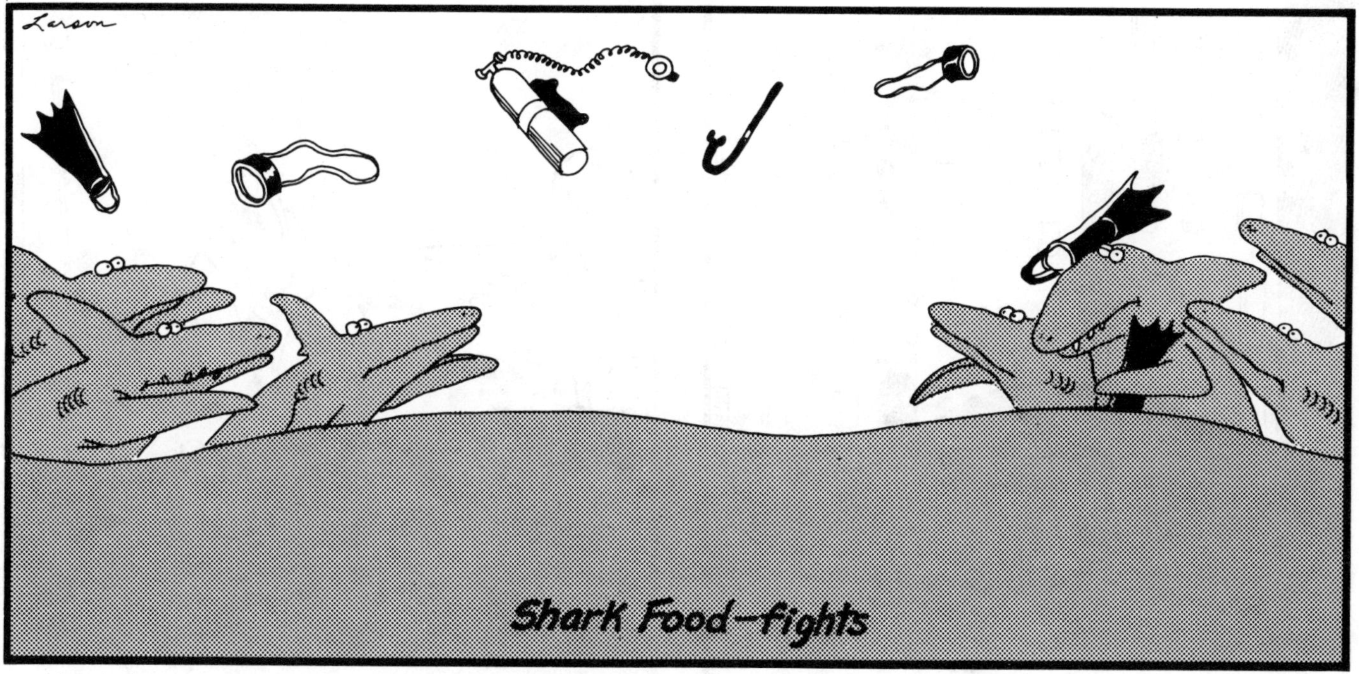
Larson
Shark Food-fights

How social animals work together

"And so I ask the jury ... is that the face of a mass murderer?"

"Hey! They're edible! ... This changes everything!"

Braving the Indian "pillow" gauntlet!

"I don't know what you're insinuating, Jane, but I haven't seen your Harold all day — besides, surely you know I would only devour my *own* husband!"

"Be firm, Arnold ... Let them in once and they'll expect it every time."

"Coincidence, ladies and gentlemen? Coincidence that my client just *happened* to live across from the A-1 Mask Co., just *happened* to walk by their office windows each day, and they, in turn, just *happened* to stumble across this new design?"

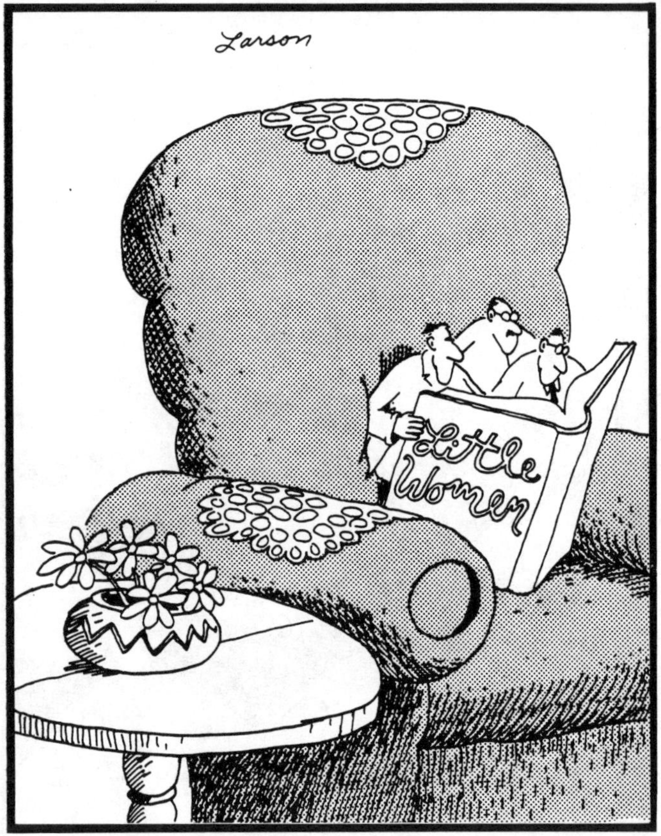
Larson
Little Women

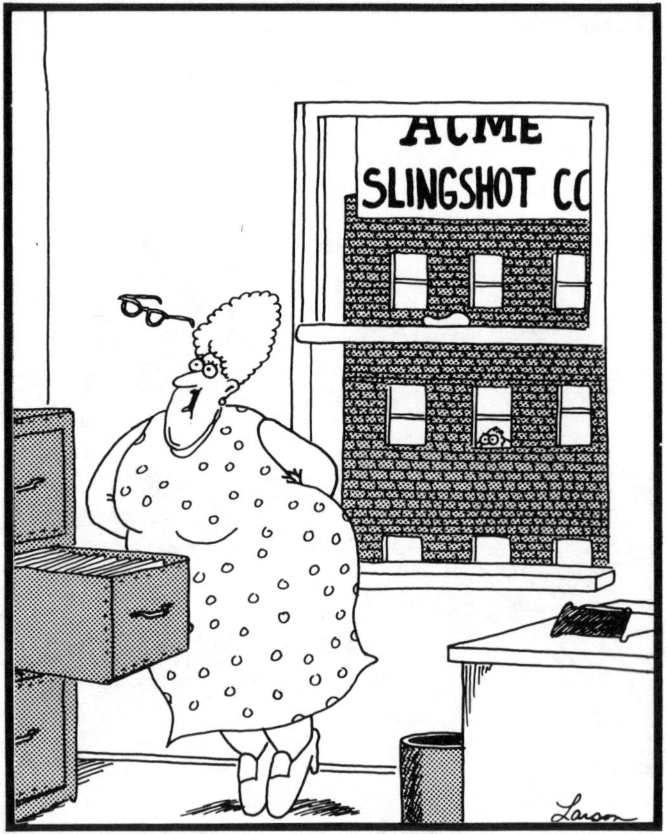
ACME
SLINGSHOT CO
Larson

"C'mon, c'mon! ... Either it's here or it isn't!"

Brain aerobics

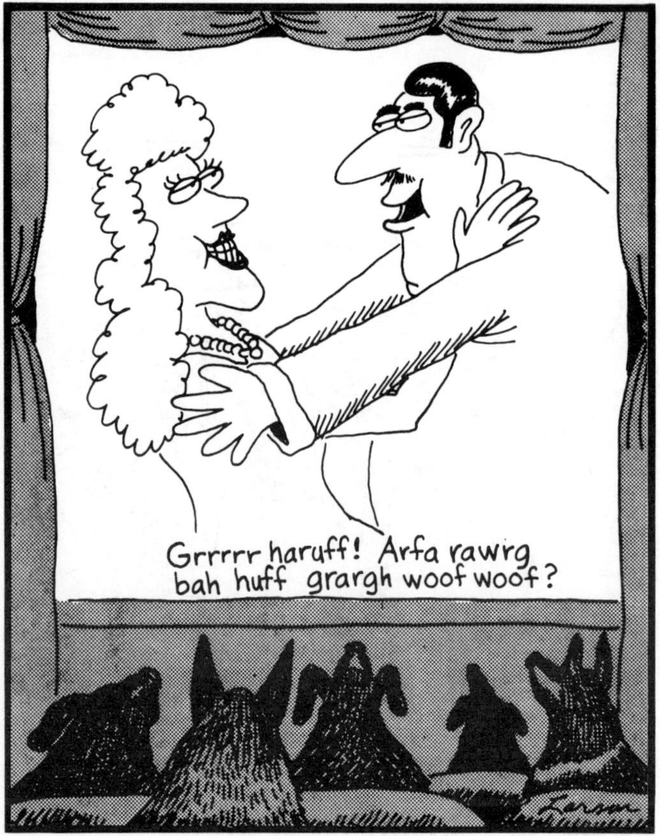
Grrrrr haruff! Arfa rawrg
bah huff grargh woof woof?
Larson

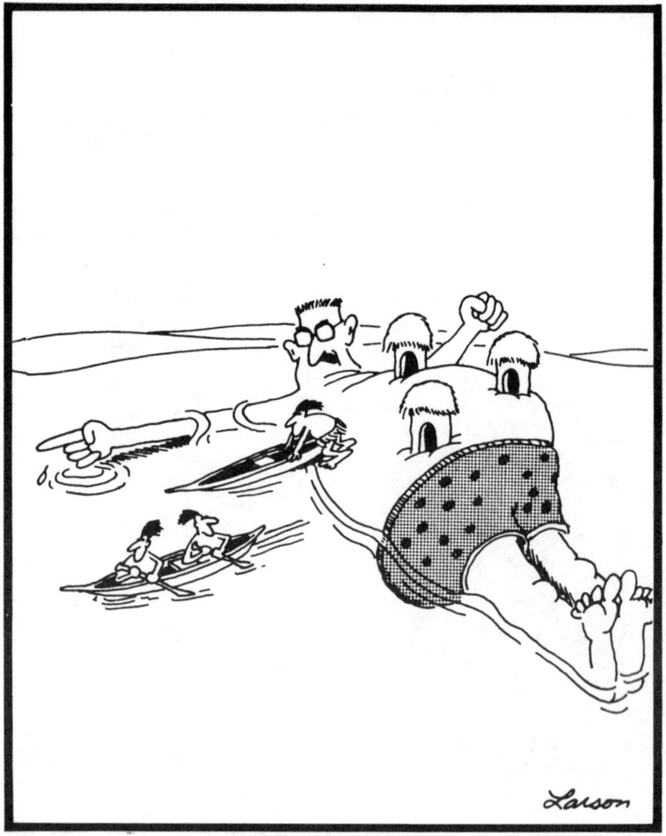
Larson

No man is an island.

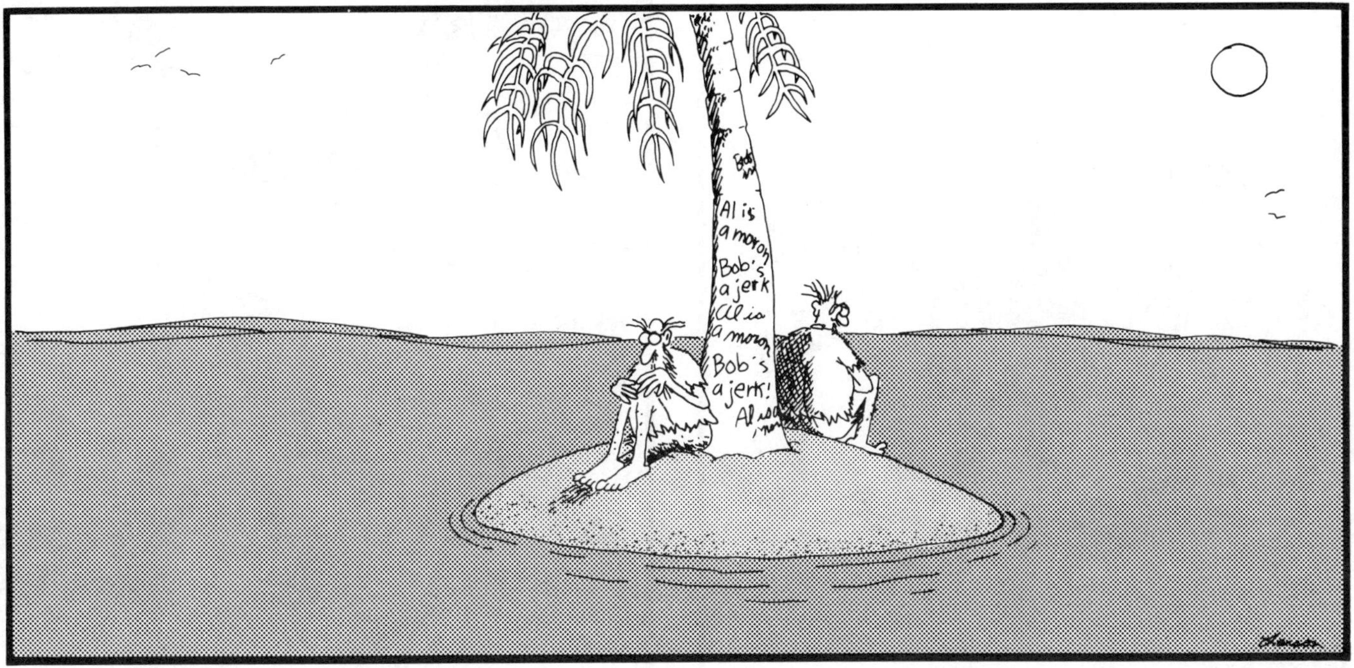
Al is
a moron
Bob's
a jerk
Al is
a moron
Bob's
a jerk!

Left to right: Old Man Winter, River, and Higgins

"Bird calls! Bird calls, you fool! ... Not mountain lions."

Gong birds

"Uh-oh, Stan ... I guess it wasn't a big, blue mule deer."

"Nuclear warheads, huh? ... More like *defused* nuclear warheads, if you ask me!"

Insectosaurs

"This is getting pretty eerie, Simmons. ... Another skull, another fortune."

"Well, one guess which table wants another round of
banana daiquiris."

"Excuse me, sir, but Shinkowsky keeps stepping
on my sandal."

Medusa starts her day.

Evening on a beached whale

Primitive mobsters

June 24, 1876: Custer's last group photo

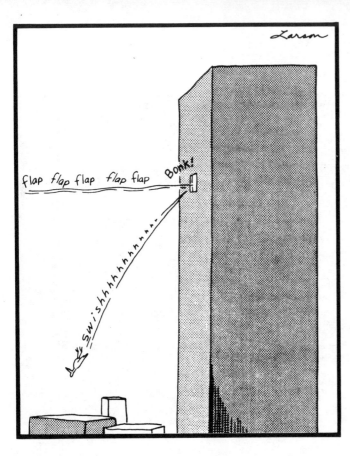

"Ohhhhhhh ... Look at that, Schuster ... Dogs are so cute when they try to comprehend quantum mechanics."

"Wheeeeeeeeeeeeeee!"

"You know what I'm sayin'? Me, for example. I couldn't
work in some stuffy little office. ... The outdoors
just calls to me."

Knowing the lions' preference for red meat, the spamalopes remained calm but wary.

"Oh please, Mom! ... I've already handled him and now the mother won't take him back."

"Oh, lovely — just the hundredth time you've managed to cut everyone's head off."

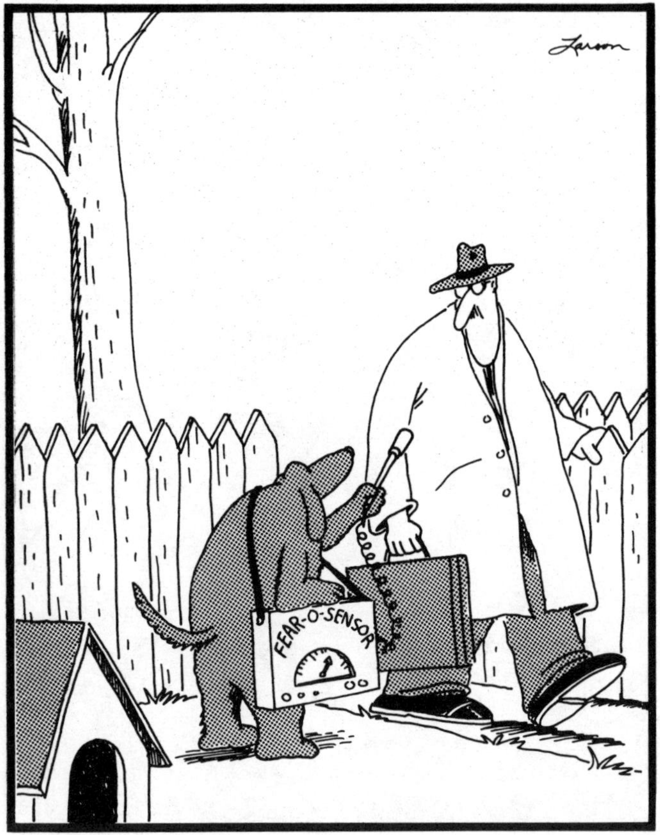
Larson
FEAR-O-SENSOR

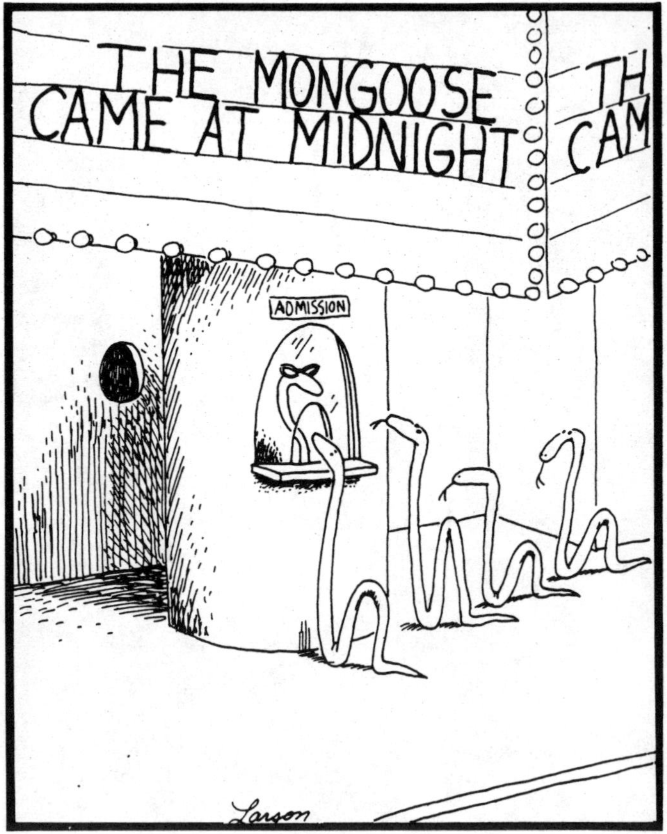
THE MONGOOSE
CAME AT MIDNIGHT
TH
CAM
ADMISSION
Larson

"OK, let's see ... That's a curse on you, a curse on you, and a curse on you."

Group photo disasters

"One bee! ... One lousy little bee gets inside and you
just lose it!"

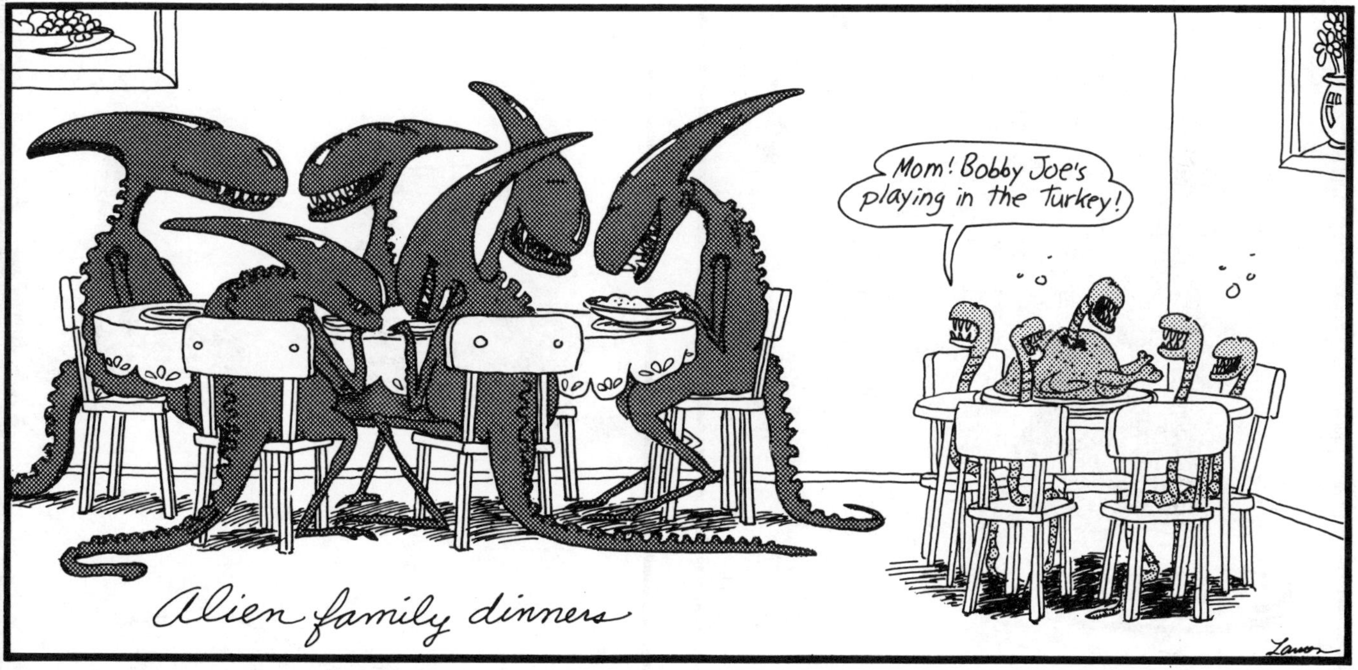
Mom! Bobby Joe's playing in the turkey!

Alien family dinners

As the first duck kept Margaret's attention, the second one made its move.

"I wonder if you could help me ... I'm looking for 523 West Cherry and ... Oh! Wow! Deja vu!"

The birth of jazz

79

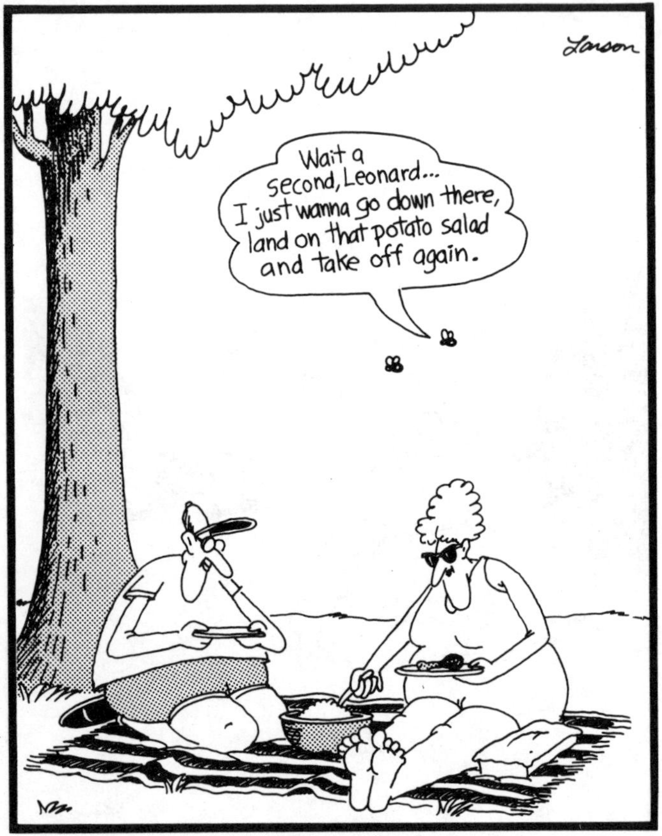
Larson
Wait a second, Leonard... I just wanna go down there, land on that potato salad and take off again.

Fly whimsy

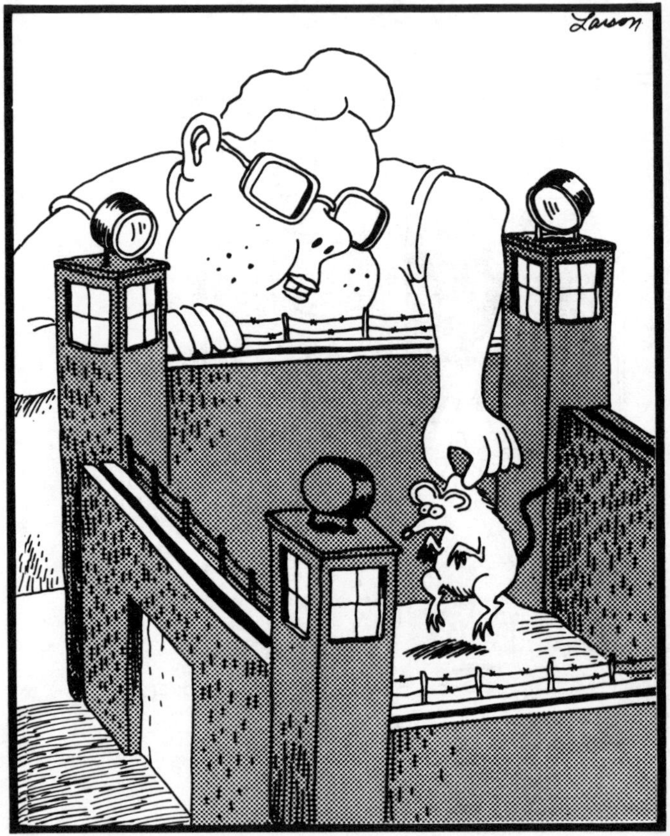
Larson

"MY reflection? Look at YOURS, Randy ... You look like some big fat swamp thing."

"Mr. Mathews! Mr. Mathews! I just came back from the restroom and Hodges here took my seat! ... It's my turn for the window seat, Mr. Mathews!"

"Quick, Abdul! Desert! ... One 's' or two?"

The Grim Reaper as a child

Witch doctor waiting rooms

Places never to set your electric eel

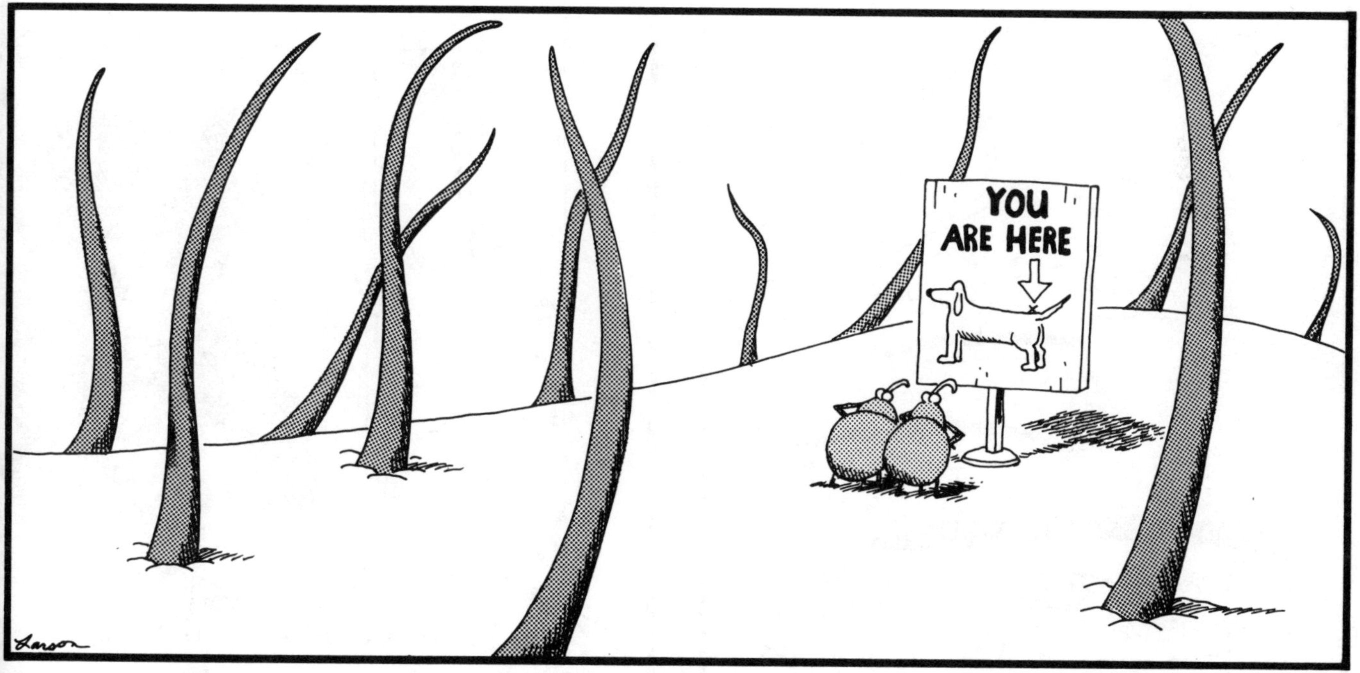
YOU
ARE HERE
Larson

50,000 B.C.: Gak Eisenberg invents the first and last silent mammoth whistle.

Roberta takes on a dust rhino.

African rakesnake

"Dang, if it doesn't happen every time! ... We just sit down
to relax and someone's knockin' at the door."

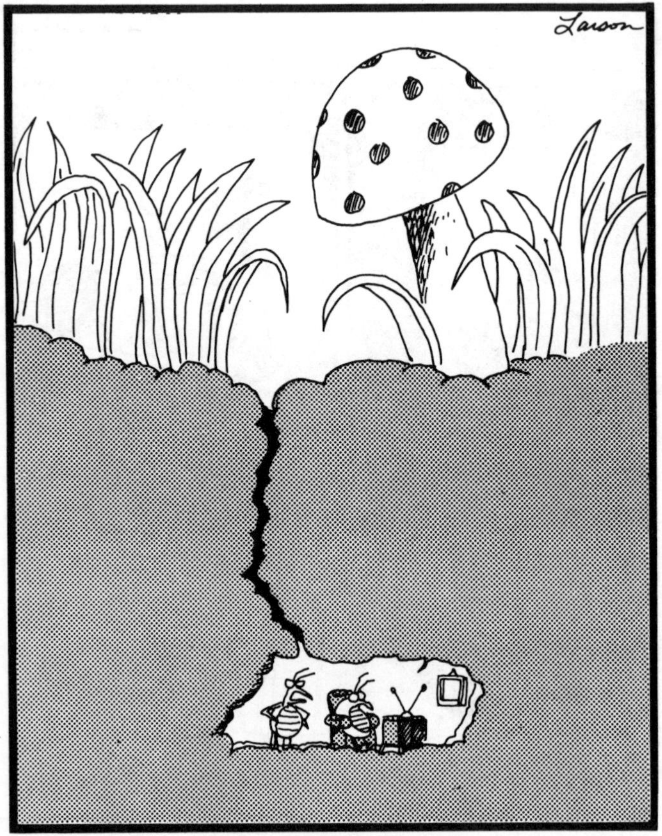
Larson

"You call this a niche?"

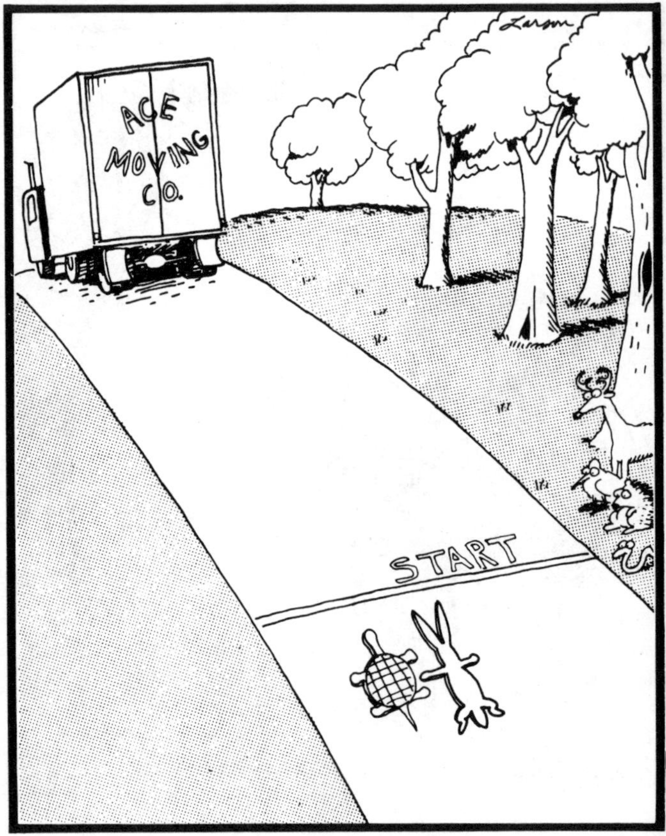
Larson
ACE
MOVING
CO.
START

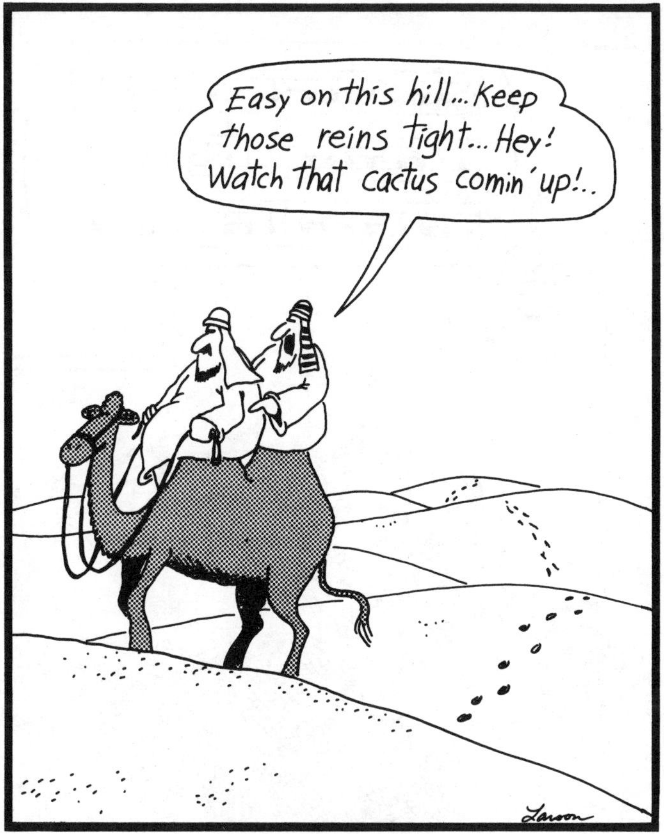
Easy on this hill... Keep those reins tight... Hey! Watch that cactus comin' up!..
Larson

Back-hump drivers

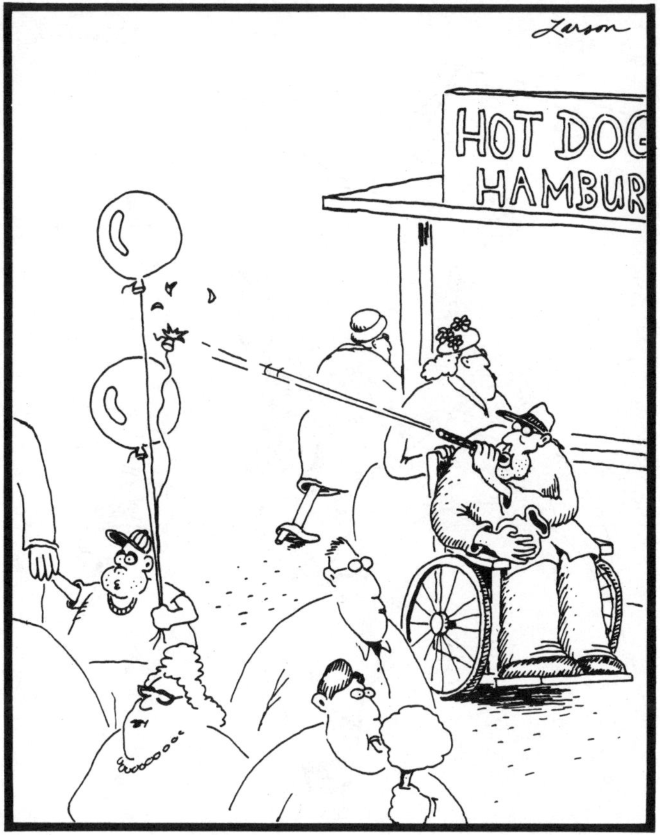
Larson
HOT DOG
HAMBUR

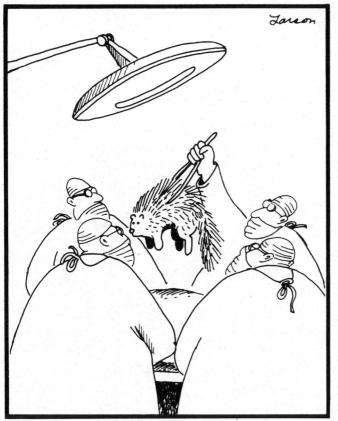

"Well, I guess that explains the abdominal pains."

"Hit the bird, Ruth — he's stuck."

"Bummer of a birthmark, Hal."

"OK, folks! ... It's a wrap!"

"Sidney, just take one ... Don't handle every fly."

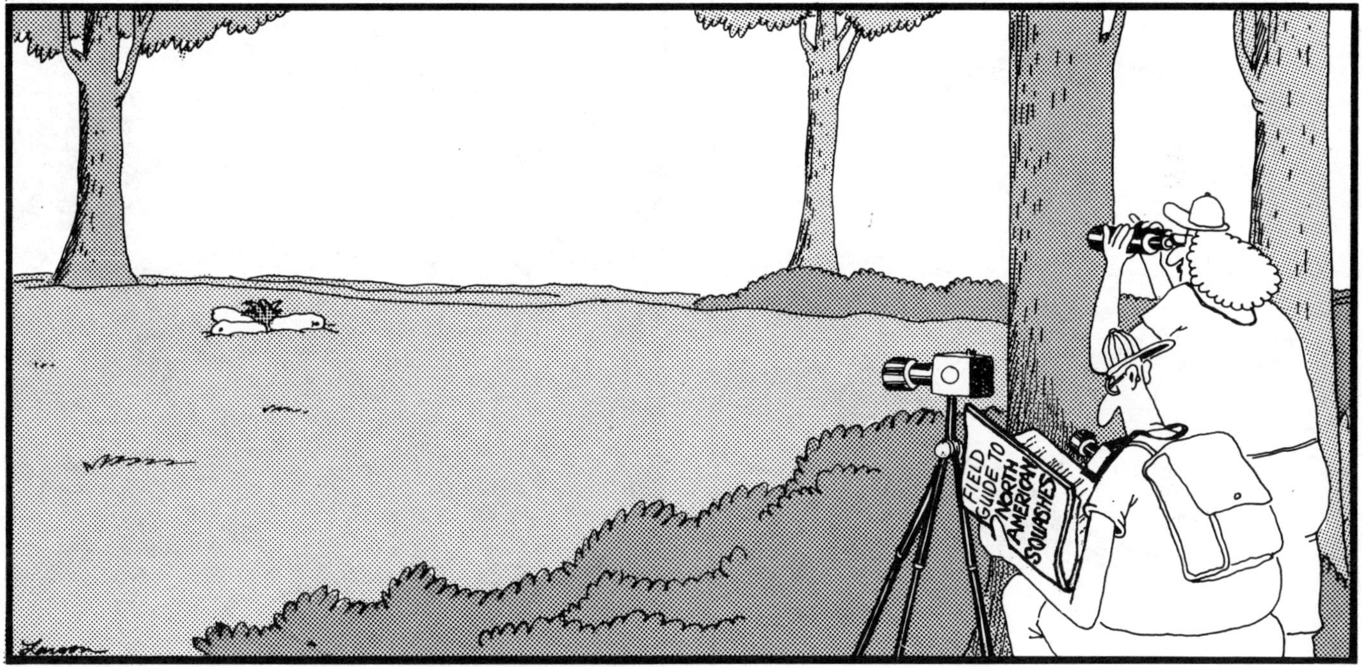
FIELD GUIDE TO NORTH AMERICAN SQUASHES

"I heard that, Simmons! I'm a wimp, am I? ... Well, to heck with you — to heck with *all* of you!"

"Hey, Bob wants in — does anyone know how to work this thing?"

"Hold it right there, Frank! ... If you're gonna shake, you do it in another room!"

"OK, guys, let's move in on those three heifers in the corner. ... Bob, you take the 'Triple R,' Dale, you take the 'Circle L,' and I'll take the 'Lazy Q.'"

Parents of a lazy river

16th-century Mona wanna-bes

"Oh, and here's Luanne now. ... Bobby just got sheared today, Luanne."

Neither rain nor snow nor sleet nor hail, they said, could stop the mail. ... But they didn't figure on Rexbo.

"Listen. We may be young, but we're in love, and we're getting married — I'll just work until Jerry pupates."

"Criminy! ... It seems like every summer there's more and more of these things around!"

"In the wild, of course, they'd be natural enemies. They do just fine together if you get 'em as pups."

"Buffalo breath? *Buffalo* breath? ... Shall we discuss your incessant little *grunting* noises?"

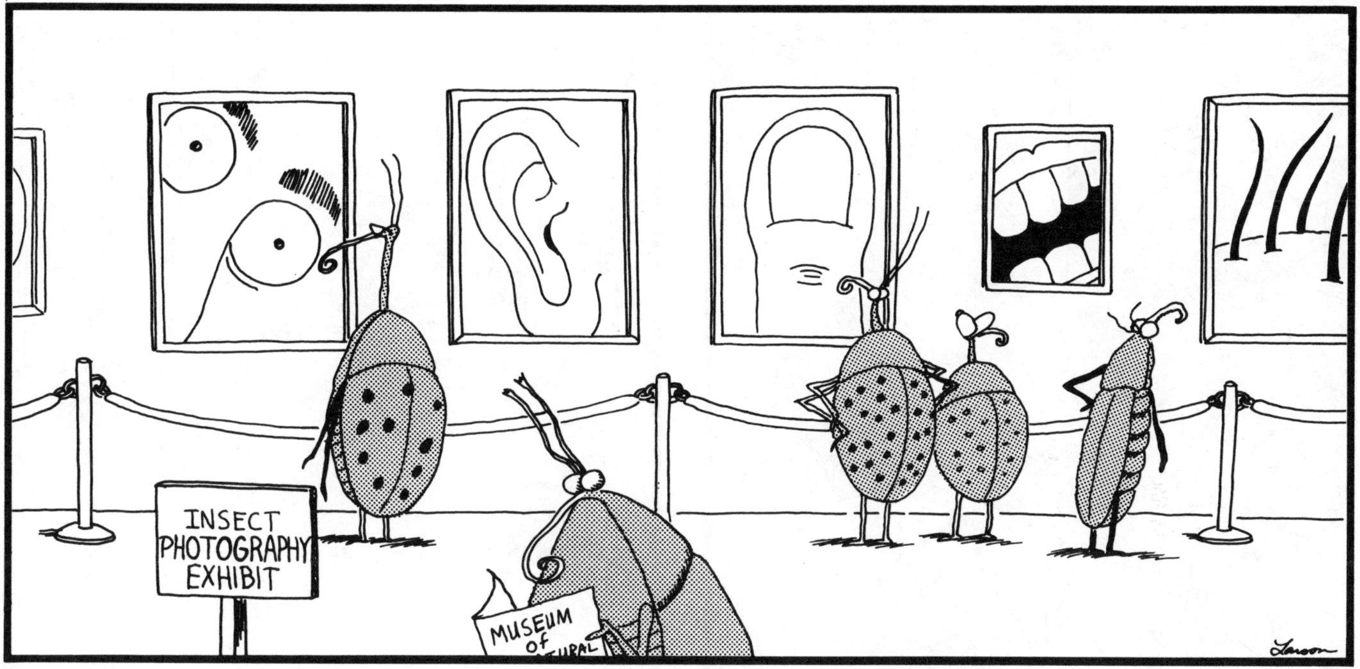
INSECT PHOTOGRAPHY EXHIBIT
MUSEUM of
Larson

The last thing a fly ever sees

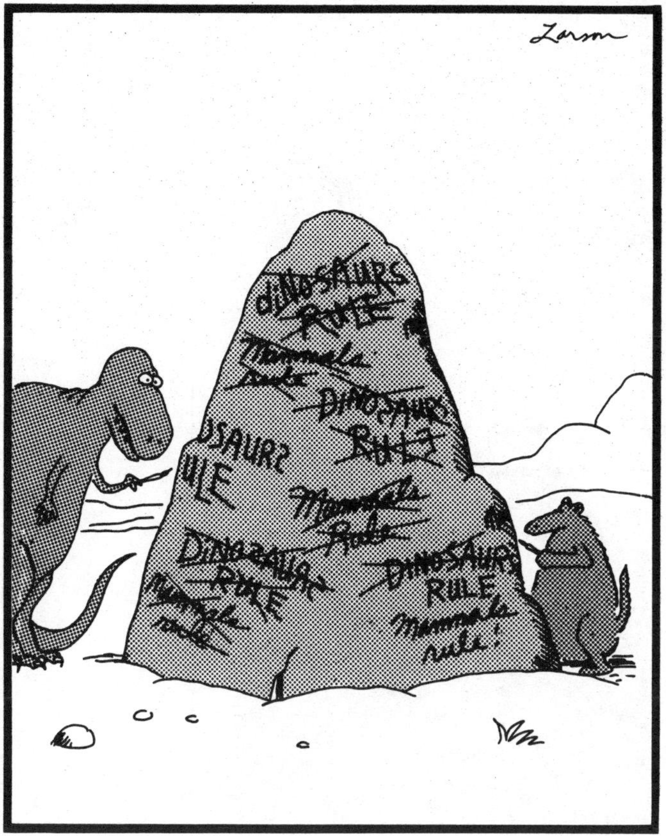
Larson
diNOSAURS RULE
DINOSAURS RULE
DINOSAURS RULE
Mammals rule!

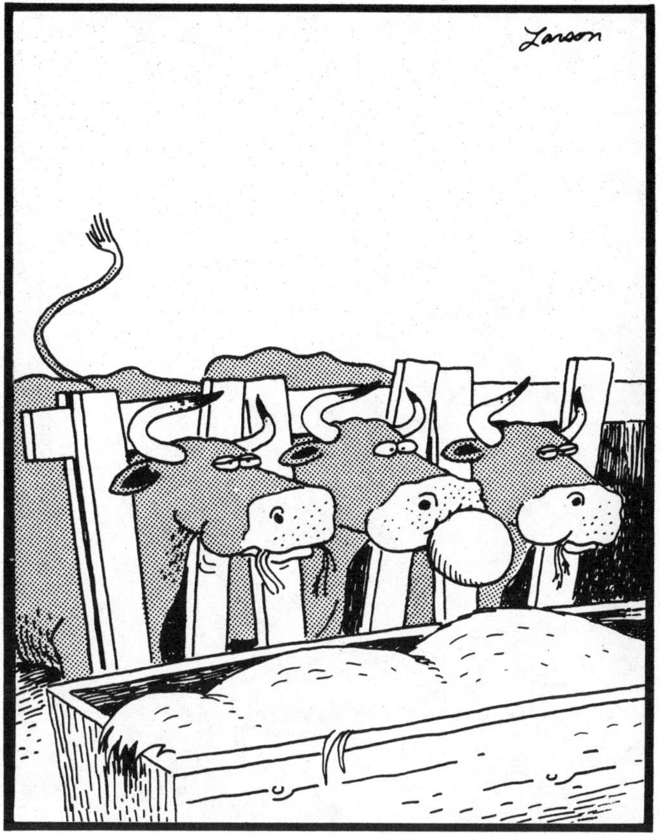
Larson

"OK, sir, would you like inferno or non-inferno? ... Ha! Just kidding. It's all inferno, of course — I just get a kick out of saying that."

"And that's the hand that fed me."